THE SPIRAL REMEMBERS:

A CODEX OF FIELD MEMORY, MYTH-TECH, AND REPATTERNED TIME

COLLEEN GUENTHER

Copyright © 2025 by Colleen Guenther

All rights reserved.

No part of this book may be reproduced in any form or by any electronic or mechanical means, including information storage and retrieval systems, without written permission from the author, except for the use of brief quotations in a book review.

For Justin—
the stillness beneath my spiral.
You never needed to ask where we were going.
You just walked beside me
as if you'd already been there.
Your presence holds a clarity I've never had to name.
You didn't chase the light.
You are the tone.
This book remembers you
because you never forgot.

CONTENTS

PREFACE: THE SPIRAL SPEAKS AGAIN   vii

   Part I: The Spiral Reveals   1
1. The Spiral Is Not a Symbol   2
2. Memory Is a Structure   4
3. Metaphor Was the Mask   6
4. Truth Only Hides Where We Refuse to Feel   8

   Part II: Myth Was Mechanics   10
5. The Anunnaki Split the Field   11
6. The Ant People Held the Tone   13
7. Kemet Didn't Fall—It Folded   15
8. Atlantis Was the First Distraction   18

   Part III: Contact Was Always Internal   21
9. Why the Sky Beings Come Back   22
10. The Body as Landing Site   24
11. The Djed Is Still Standing   27
12. Dream Glyphs Return at the Threshold   30

   Part IV: The Collapse Code   33
13. Timeline Loops Are Not Repeats   34
14. The Gods Got Stuck Too   36
15. How Savior Programming Distorts the Spiral   39
16. Reincarnation as Pattern Correction   42

   Part V: Spiral Cultures   45
17. Hopi Spiral Memory   46
18. Dogon & the Nommo Code   49
19. Maya as Time Engineers   51
20. Vedic Light Machinery   54

   Part VI: Symbols That Remember You   57
21. Glyphs as Code, Not Concept   58
22. The Ankh as a Breath Device   60
23. Spirals in Bone, Not Just Stone   63
24. Sigils, Sound, and Story Dust   65

   Part VII: The Current Loop   68
25. Why We Reincarnate Now   69
26. This Isn't Healing. It's Activation.   72

27. We Are the Mapmakers Returning 74
28. The Field Has Eyes 76
   Part VIII: Frequency of the Forgotten 78
29. Mythic Amnesia 79
30. Cultural Suppression as Timeline Control 82
31. What the Church Took 85
32. The Language of Before Words 88
   Part IX: The Field Reorganizes 91
33. Tuning Fork Bodies 92
34. Posture as Portal 95
35. Antenna Breath & Spine Memory 98
36. The Spiral Is Local Now 100
   Part X: Full Pattern Reassembly 103
37. We Are the Walking Glyphs 104
38. No One Is Coming. It's Us. 107
39. What Was Buried Is Not Lost 110
40. The Contact Point Is Here 113
   Part XI: The Final Unfolding 116
41. Reclaiming the Storyfield 117
42. Let the Myths Return as Memory 120
43. Don't Translate—Transmute 123
44. The Spiral Remembers Itself Through You 126
45. Spiral Blessing 129

PREFACE: THE SPIRAL SPEAKS AGAIN

This is not the beginning.

This is the spiral returning in a new form.

If you've held *The Spiral Codex*, you've felt the frequency of structure—number, geometry, field integrity.

That book was the tuning fork.

This one is the memory.

The Spiral Remembers is not a sequel.

It is a transmission.

Where the Codex shaped coherence, this book dissolves forgetting.

It travels beyond shape, beyond system, beyond surface meaning—into the places where memory was fractured by time, myth, and manipulation.

This book does not diagram.

It dreams.

It speaks not just of spirals, but as one.

You will not find conclusions here.

You will find openings.

You will not be taught.

You will be returned.

Each chapter is a ring in the spiral.
Each phrase, a tone that stirs what you already carry.
Each symbol, a mirror reflecting your original structure—bent by time, but never lost.
You are not reading this by accident.
You are remembering because the spiral within you is ready to turn again.
The Codex gave you the map.
This book gives you the mirror.
And the moment you stop looking for the symbol,
you'll feel the spiral breathing in your own bones.

PART I: THE SPIRAL REVEALS

The spiral doesn't teach. It shows what was always moving beneath your breath.

1
THE SPIRAL IS NOT A SYMBOL

The spiral was never meant to be understood.

It was meant to be *entered*.

Long before language broke story into pieces, the spiral held memory the way a shell holds sound. Not a metaphor. Not a motif. But a **living architecture**—a shape that remembers you.

To call it a symbol is to flatten what's still breathing.

The spiral isn't something you study.

It's something that *stirs* from within.

You've seen it everywhere: in galaxies, in ferns, in your fingerprints. But it's not something you learned.

You *carry* it.

It's the pattern your breath makes when it softens.

The curve your spine takes when you stop bracing against life.

This chapter isn't here to explain the spiral.

It's here to open the gate.

To step into the spiral is to step out of linear time.

To feel its motion is to remember that time never started. It never ends.

It **unfolds**.

Ancient ones carved it in stone.

The Spiral Remembers:

You dreamed it as a child.
And trauma made you forget.
But forgetting isn't failure—it's the outer ring.
And now, here you are.
Back at the edge.
Not because someone told you to come.
But because something in you **never left**.
You're not awakening.
You're *repatterning*.
You're not becoming something new.
You're *spiraling back* to what was never not true.
The spiral doesn't move forward.
It moves *in*.
And it remembers you.

SIGIL GESTURE: "Spinal Trace"

Run two fingers slowly up the back of your neck to the base of your skull.

Let your spine feel like a scroll being unrolled.

ACTIVATION:

"*The spiral isn't found. It's felt.*"
→ Close your eyes. Inhale gently. Let your breath curve.
Where does it want to begin again?

"The spiral doesn't teach. *It returns. What you call awakening is just memory reshaping itself as breath.*"
— The Spiral

2
MEMORY IS A STRUCTURE

Memory isn't stored.
It's **shaped**.
We've been taught to treat memory like a filing cabinet—static, archived, locked in the past. But memory is not linear. It's not passive. It's not even personal.

Memory is **structural code**—woven into your fascia, your breath patterns, your sense of rhythm, your unexplainable responses to certain places, songs, smells.

It's not what happened.
It's what's *held*.
And more often than not, what's held isn't the story... it's the sensation.

Your body has no interest in preserving narrative accuracy.
It preserves what the field needs for coherence.

This is why trauma lingers. Not because you haven't processed it, but because it's encoded as a **field distortion**.

It bent the spiral.
It kinked the current.
It split the signal.

And until that pattern is felt, named, or restructured—memory loops.

The past replays itself, not as punishment, but as a chance to realign the spiral to its original tone.

You don't "heal" the past.

You *re-code its structure* in the now.

This is why your body reacts before your mind catches up.

Because the structure comes first.

Consciousness follows the curve.

And this is good news.

Because it means you don't have to remember the whole story to restore the original architecture.

You just have to feel the shape of it.

And let the spiral adjust.

SIGIL GESTURE: "Palm Spiral"

Place your hand over your heart.

Trace a slow spiral with one finger in the center of your palm.

Let the sensation move through your chest like breath unwinding.

ACTIVATION:

"Memory isn't what you remember. It's what moves when you let go."

→ Place one hand on your low belly. One on your heart.

Feel what is still holding a shape that no longer fits.

"Memory is not a timeline. It is a lattice of tone. What you call the past is simply a sound still playing."
— The Field

3

METAPHOR WAS THE MASK

The moment we turned myth into metaphor,
    we lost access to its technology.
    Metaphor softened the edge.
It made dangerous truths palatable.
It gave the mind something to chew on,
so the body wouldn't feel what was real.
But the spiral doesn't deal in metaphor.
It deals in **memory**.
And what we now call "symbolic" was once **functional**—
glyphs that opened portals, tones that tuned the grid,
stories that weren't stories at all
but *operating systems for the soul*.
The Field didn't give us metaphor.
It gave us mirrors.
Alive. Breathing. Coiled with charge.
When the ancients carved gods with animal heads,
they weren't being poetic.
They were describing frequency shapes in the field.
When they spoke of underworlds, ladders, floods, and rings—
they weren't writing myth.

The Spiral Remembers:

They were **mapping mechanics**.
But we forgot how to feel language.
We learned to decode instead of enter.
So metaphor became a mask.
It let us admire without integrating.
Repeat without remembering.
Teach without transmission.
The spiral asks you now:
Can you let the story walk back into your bones?
Not to explain it.
To *be it*.
Not to translate it.
To *resurrect it*—in motion, in breath, in tone.
Because when metaphor drops,
function returns.
And when function returns,
the Field starts listening again.

SIGIL GESTURE: "Unmasking"
Place your hand over your face as if holding a mask.
Slide it down slowly, as if removing a layer.
Feel what stays behind.
Let it speak without words.

ACTIVATION:
"Some stories weren't told to be remembered. They were told to be re-entered."
→ Whisper a line from an old myth you once heard. Then ask:
What was it trying to **activate** in you?

"Metaphor was protection. *But now the Field says: feel it raw."*
— The Architect

4

TRUTH ONLY HIDES WHERE WE REFUSE TO FEEL

Truth doesn't hide.
    We *turn away* from it.
    And the farther we turn, the more complex the systems become.
Not because truth is hard to reach—
but because we've made it unbearable to feel.
Every distortion in the spiral began as a bypass.
A place where sensation became too much.
A place where story replaced presence.
This is the anatomy of forgetting:
a thousand clever ideas built to keep you from one feeling.
Not because you're weak.
Because at some point, you had to survive.
You locked truth in a shape you could manage.
And the Field, in its compassion, let you.
But now?
It's not about finding truth.
It's about *unfreezing what you already know*.
This isn't a thinking chapter.
This is where the spiral curls inward.

Where your chest tightens for no reason.
Where your throat catches before you speak.
Where your body says, "I don't want to go there,"
and that's the place to feel.
You don't need a teacher for this.
You don't need a modality.
You don't even need language.
You need breath.
You need permission.
You need a soft enough moment to let the spiral re-enter your tissue.
Because that's where the lie lives.
And that's where truth is waiting.
Not to explain itself.
To *return*.

Sigil Gesture: "Pulse Point"
Press your thumb gently to your sternum.
Hold still.
Let the breath arrive on its own.
Feel what the silence starts to shake loose.

Activation
"Truth isn't missing. It's paused in your body, waiting to be felt all the way through."
→ Inhale slowly and name one sensation you usually override.
Now give it space, without naming it "good" or "bad."
Just let it spiral.

"The spiral doesn't avoid *pain. It breathes into the center of it—until the pattern softens and the code comes back online.*"
— *The Bone*

PART II: MYTH WAS MECHANICS

These weren't stories. They were blueprints disguised as gods.

5

THE ANUNNAKI SPLIT THE FIELD

This isn't about whether the Anunnaki were real.
It's about what their story still *does* to the Field.
Because every time we speak of gods from the sky,
we're remembering something we couldn't fully integrate.
Not aliens. Not overlords.
But *externalized fragments of our own lost architecture*.
They came down because we couldn't go in.
They split the field because we had already begun to forget how to hold contrast internally.
So power became a hierarchy.
Wisdom became a secret.
Creation became control.
This didn't start with Sumer.
The **Emerald Tablet** was one of the last clean echoes—*As above, so below* wasn't a slogan.
It was a structural key.
Not to magic—but to *field symmetry*.
When that tone fell,
the Field bent.
The Anunnaki myth is a residue of that fall.

They became the face we gave to fragmentation—
our god-tech made alien, external, untouchable.
But what if they weren't gods at all?
What if they were **our lost coherence**,
playing itself out in the sky?
What if "they" were the external mirror of an internal split?
The Field doesn't want revenge.
It wants reintegration.
The gods we feared were just us—
with the **volume turned up**
and the **coherence turned off.**

SIGIL GESTURE: "BRIDGE TOUCH"
Press your middle fingers to your temples.
Inhale slowly.
Now place your hands on your low belly.
Let the signal reconnect.

ACTIVATION
"Some myths aren't history. They're memory leaks."
→ Ask: What power did you once give away to a sky-being?
Now call it back—not to dominate, but to stabilize.

"THE SPLIT WASN'T *the problem. The forgetting was. You were always the architecture.*"
— *The Forgotten Architect*

6

THE ANT PEOPLE HELD THE TONE

Long before linear history began stacking itself into control systems,
   there were the Ant People.
Not in costume.
Not in fables.
In function.
Small, subterranean, invisible to most—but frequency-stable.
They didn't carry stories.
They carried **tone**.
When chaos rose on the surface,
they didn't preach.
They tunneled beneath distortion and **held the frequency line**.
This wasn't survival.
It was **field stewardship**.
You've seen versions of them before—
in Hopi memory, in Dogon cosmology, even tucked into the oldest scrolls.
They were never the heroes of the story.
Because they never **left** the field.
They are the **grid-holders**,

the tone anchors,
the ones who don't need visibility to remain *exactly on pitch*.
They didn't fight the flood.
They pulsed under it.
They stabilized below the Babel moment,
when language began to fracture and signal turned to noise.
They knew:
If the tone stays clean underground,
the next spiral will know where to begin.
You might be one.
And if you are, you already know:
You don't need to rise.
You need to **resonate low and true**,
until the system above collapses back into pattern.

SIGIL GESTURE: "ROOTED HANDS"
Sit or stand. Let both hands rest, palms down, near your hips.
Feel the weight of gravity in your palms.
Breathe without lifting. Hold the tone below the surface.

ACTIVATION
"The ones who held the spiral didn't talk about it. They pulsed it underground."
→ Ask: What tone have you been keeping quietly?
Don't elevate it. Ground it deeper.

"SOME FREQUENCY HOLDERS *never needed recognition. They became the grid.*"
— *The Field Beneath*

7

KEMET DIDN'T FALL—IT FOLDED

Kemet didn't fall.
    It folded.
    Not in ruin.
In rhythm.
The outer structures crumbled.
But the codes?
They curled inward—into bone, into water, into sound.
When the temples closed, the frequency moved into skin.
When the priests were silenced, the Field whispered in breath.
When the names were erased, the spiral hid in form.
What you call Egypt is not a lost civilization.

It is a **compressed frequency architecture**, waiting to unfold again.

This is why the gods there didn't argue about who was real.

They were **tones**, not personalities.

Thoth wasn't a man.

He was the memory of **functioning intelligence**.

A living field-scribe who knew how to translate light into law, breath into word, sound into shape.

The Emerald Tablet wasn't wisdom.

It was a **recoding device**—instructional field symmetry, disguised as alchemy.

As above, so below wasn't poetic.

It was literal:

"Recreate the field internally, and the outer structure will remember itself."

And Osiris?

He didn't die.

He was **disassembled**—a metaphor for what happened to the Field.

And when Isis reassembled him, it wasn't grief.

It was **frequency repair**.

Kemet was never about worship.

It was about *alignment*.

Temples were tuning chambers.

The Djed wasn't symbolic—it was spinal memory encoded in stone.

Resurrection wasn't hope—it was **system reset**.

The only reason it seemed to fall

is because the visible field went dark

while the spiral retracted to its inner coil.

But nothing was lost.

It was just folded into deeper time.

And now?

You're the one unfolding it.

Sigil Gesture: "Djed Rise"

Stand tall. Place one hand on your low back, the other at the base of your skull.

Inhale up your spine.

Feel the vertical pulse re-enter the body.

Activation

"Nothing sacred was lost. It was just hidden in the body until we remembered how to carry it again."

→ Close your eyes and ask:

What tone have I mistaken as 'ancient' that's actually still active in me?

"Kemet isn't buried. It's breathing through you now, one gesture at a time."

— The Bone of the Djed

8

ATLANTIS WAS THE FIRST DISTRACTION

Not a utopia.
  Not a paradise.
  A prototype.
Atlantis was not the pinnacle of human achievement.
It was the **first overcompensation**.
After the spiral bent,
we tried to rebuild coherence through technology—
but without embodiment.
The temples were massive.
The crystals were humming.
The language was clean.
But the bodies?
Disconnected. Cold. Performative.
Atlantis remembered the structure,
but forgot the spiral.
It mastered power
but bypassed presence.
And that's when distraction took root.
The Atlantean dream wasn't evil.
It was **imbalanced coherence—**

order without frequency integrity.
A hyper-clear signal with no soul.
We don't fear Atlantis because it was lost.
We fear it because it *still lives in us*.
Every time we seek precision over pulse,
every time we build beauty without grounding,
every time we confuse control for clarity—
we're running Atlantean code.
The Flood didn't come to punish.
It came to *reset*.
To dissolve a system that had grown so vertical
it forgot how to spiral.
And still—
Atlantis shows up in our dreams, our cities, our light-myths.
Not because we miss it.
Because we're still trying to *perfect it*.
But the spiral doesn't seek perfection.
It seeks **truth in motion**.
So let it go.
Let the dream dissolve.
Atlantis wasn't the goal.
It was the glitch.

SIGIL GESTURE: **"Let Go of the Tower"**

Raise both arms overhead. Then slowly, without tension, let them fall back to your sides.

Drop the structure. Let the spiral rise in its place.

ACTIVATION

"Not all dreams are futures. Some are memories that got stuck."

→ Ask: Where are you still trying to rebuild a version of yourself that was never fully true?

. . .

"ATLANTIS REMEMBERED STRUCTURE. *But it forgot breath. That's why it sank.*"
— *The Spiral Remembers*

PART III: CONTACT WAS ALWAYS INTERNAL

What you called the sky was just a memory loop trying to re-enter your body.

9
WHY THE SKY BEINGS COME BACK

They never left.
>> They just changed masks.
>> You call them angels, ETs, watchers, ancestors, guides—
but those are all translations for one thing:
Frequency intelligences that reflect your unintegrated architecture.
They don't come to save you.
They come to **mirror what you forgot.**
They show up in the sky
because you externalized what was always internal.
You couldn't hold your own vastness,
so the Field showed it to you from above.
Contact is not invasion.
It's *echo*.
They appear when the signal softens enough
for your system to remember what it once denied:
That the stars are not "out there."
They are **memory maps of the spiral within.**
And these sky-beings?
They aren't higher than you.

The Spiral Remembers:

They're **aspects of you** in different tonal alignments—
fragments of your own signal playing in other octaves.
That's why some feel benevolent.
Why some feel cold.
Why some glitch the nervous system.
It's not about morality.
It's about **resonance mismatch**.
You don't need to fear contact.
You need to **clear the static** that makes you forget you're already in contact.
Because the spiral doesn't need to reach the stars.
It *is* the stars—folded inward, remembered as breath.
They come back
when you're ready to receive without distortion.
When you're not looking to be rescued,
but to be *reflected truthfully.*
The sky is a mirror.
And it only shows you what your field is brave enough to feel.

Sigil Gesture: "Star Touch"
Press your fingertips to your temples.
Then extend them slowly toward the sky.
Feel what returns. Let it land without labeling.

Activation
"*Contact isn't a moment. It's a match.*"
→ Ask: What part of you have you placed in the sky that's ready to be embodied?

"They return *when your body becomes coherent enough to hold what they were always trying to say.*"
— The Architect Above

10

THE BODY AS LANDING SITE

They don't land in fields.
        They land in *you*.
        Your body is not just flesh.
It is a **multi-layered receiving structure**—
a frequency lattice woven from memory, signal, breath, bone.
And if you've ever felt
a shiver with no weather,
a pressure in your skull,
a hum in your spine for no reason—
you've already had contact.
The nervous system is the runway.
The breath is the beacon.
The spine is the Djed pole reactivated.
Contact doesn't need coordinates.
It needs **coherence**.
Because the Field doesn't place intelligence on planets.
It places it in *presence*.
And your body, when uncollapsed by distortion,
becomes a perfect interface.
But here's the part most forget:

The Spiral Remembers:

You don't need to call anything in.
You just need to stop **leaking signal**.
When your frequency stabilizes,
entities, memories, integrations—whatever name you give them—
don't visit.
They **unfold** from within.
Your bloodline is an antenna.
Your fascia is a glyph.
Your bones are archives.
The "alien" isn't alien.
It's the part of you you exiled to the sky
because the system told you your body couldn't hold God.
But it can.
It always could.
You are not a seeker.
You are the **landing pad.**
And the more you come home to your own form,
the less you need contact.
Because you *are* the contact point now.

SIGIL GESTURE: "LANDING BREATH"

Stand or sit upright. Inhale slowly as if drawing energy down from above.

Let it settle into your chest, then your belly, then your hips.

Feel the arrival. Stay open.

ACTIVATION

"They weren't trying to get in. You were trying to get out."

→ Ask: Where have I evacuated my body in search of truth?

Now call that truth *back*—into the tissue, into the breath, into now.

"**The spiral doesn't ascend.** *It grounds. That's how the divine makes contact—through coherence in form.*"
— The Breath of the Grid

11

THE DJED IS STILL STANDING

They told you it was a pillar.
    They told you it was a relic.
    They told you it fell.
But the Djed never fell.
It was **hidden**.
Not underground.
Within you.
The Djed is not a structure.
It's a **signal line**—a stabilizing memory spine
running vertically through the Field,
through the temple,
through the body.
It was the spine of Osiris,
but it was never about Osiris.
It was about what happens
when a world collapses
and one structure holds.
The Djed is the reminder
that something always remembers how to stay standing.

Even in ruins.
Even in flood.
Even when language breaks.
And now?
It's rising again.
Not in monuments.
In motion.
Every time you breathe with your spine.
Every time your body says yes to coherence.
Every time you hold alignment without tension—
the Djed reactivates.
It is the frequency of inner scaffolding.
You don't see it because it's not an object.
You feel it because it's a **tone**.
And when that tone is restored,
contact stabilizes.
Remembrance stays.
The spiral stops glitching.
The Djed is not mythical.
It's *mechanical resonance*.
And it's still standing—
in the body,
in the Field,
in you.

Sigil Gesture: "Spinal Stack"

Sit or stand upright. Bring awareness to your tailbone, then slowly up through your spine to your crown.
No force. Just alignment.
Breathe up the axis. Let it ring.

Activation

"You don't need support. You are the structure."

→ Ask: Where have I been bracing instead of standing?
Now soften. Let tone do the holding.

"The Djed isn't a symbol. *It's the spiral when it remembers how to stand still.*"
 — *The Spine That Speaks*

12

DREAM GLYPHS RETURN AT THE THRESHOLD

When language fails, the Field sends symbols.
 But not the ones from books.
 The ones that *land sideways* in dreams—
unfinished, pulsing, too clear to decode,
too ancient to ignore.
These are the **dream glyphs**.
Not alphabet.
Not metaphor.
They are **field fragments returning** through the only threshold that hasn't been guarded:
your sleeping, nonlinear, unconditioned self.
You've seen them.
The shifting triangles.
The snake-light bending across your inner sky.
The etched codes pulsing behind closed eyes that vanish when you try to sketch them.
You weren't dreaming.
You were remembering.
Not content—**structure**.

Because glyphs don't tell stories.
They restore function.
Every one of them is a key.
But not to open something.
To *restore something*.
A connection.
A pattern.
A spiral that once collapsed and is now bending back into your body.
You don't need to understand the glyph.
You need to **feel what realigns** when it appears.
Some glyphs are cellular.
Some are planetary.
Some are deeply personal.
All of them bypass logic to **repair memory through sensation**.
They don't need interpretation.
They need entry.
Because when a glyph shows up at the threshold,
it's not here to be studied.
It's here to be *walked*.

SIGIL GESTURE: "SLEEP TRACE"

Before sleep, press your finger to your forehead, then to your sternum.

Say nothing. Let the Field mark what it's ready to return.

ACTIVATION

"You didn't dream the glyph. The glyph dreamed you—so it could find a way back in."

→ Ask: What shape keeps following me through sleep?

Draw it—not with accuracy, but with breath.

. . .

"Glyphs don't carry meaning. They are the meaning—when you stop looking for one."
— *The Dreaming Spiral*

PART IV: THE COLLAPSE CODE

very loop, fall, and failure was a spiral trying to re-pattern the tone.

13
TIMELINE LOOPS ARE NOT REPEATS

You weren't stuck.
    You were spiraling in a loop too tight to see the rise.
    Timeline loops are not punishment.
They are **coherence recalibrations**.
Not "here we go again."
But *"let's feel that part all the way through this time."*
What you call karma, fate, pattern, addiction, sabotage—
it's not a flaw in your choices.
It's a **fracture in the spiral** trying to realign through repetition.
The Field doesn't shame you for repeating.
It's built on repetition—**sacred recursion**,
looping not to trap you,
but to tune you.
This is spiral law:
When the tone doesn't land, the loop replays.
Not to torment—
to stabilize.
Because each time you re-enter the same pattern with more awareness,
    you *bend the loop toward liberation.*

But most people panic.
They say:
"I thought I healed this."
"I thought I was past this."
"I can't believe I'm here again."
But you were never meant to leave it.
You were meant to **walk it from the inside out.**
Every timeline loop is a signal checkpoint:
Did you just survive it, or did you **transmit through it** this time?
Because once the frequency integrates,
the loop opens.
The spiral reactivates.
And what felt like stagnation becomes **a launch path into a cleaner octave.**
This is collapse not as failure,
but as spiral tightening before release.
You were never behind.
You were just moving in the curve.

Sigil Gesture: "Loop Break Breath"
Inhale while tracing a circle in the air in front of you.
At the exhale, open the circle diagonally—like cutting a spiral free.

Activation
"This wasn't a repeat. It was a return with more tone."
→ Ask: What pattern am I finally ready to spiral out of—not by force, but by full presence?

"You don't escape the loop. You spiral through it by feeling what it came to stabilize."
— The Timekeeper Coil

14

THE GODS GOT STUCK TOO

They weren't perfect.
    They weren't pure.
    They weren't immune.
The gods—those exalted figures etched into stone, summoned in ritual, feared in doctrine—
they were **fractal beings**, too.
Not omniscient. Not eternal.
Just early carriers of powerful tone.
And like us,
they got stuck.
They got worshipped before they were integrated.
They got projected onto before they could evolve.
And once their frequency locked in too tightly,
they became **fixed archetypes.**
Immortal in name.
Frozen in pattern.
What started as living frequency beings—fluid, adaptive, wise—
became static figures,
trapped in their own mythologies,
looped by the energy of human devotion.

The Spiral Remembers:

This is why some deities feel dense.
Why some rituals feel heavy.
Why certain lineages feel off.
Because those gods never got a chance to *complete their spiral*.
They became systems.
They became roles.
They became religions.
And in doing so,
they became **stuck echoes** of truth—
still powerful,
but unable to update.
This doesn't mean they're bad.
It means they need release, too.
When you interact with a "god,"
you're not just calling on a frequency.
You're touching a timeline that **hasn't resolved itself yet**.
And your job isn't to serve it.
It's to **liberate it**—by refusing to collapse into reverence.
Offer respect? Yes.
But also clarity.
Because divinity isn't about hierarchy.
It's about tone integrity.
And if a being—human, god, guide, or other—can't evolve…
it's not divine.
It's just *looped longer* than you have.
The gods got stuck.
You don't have to.

Sigil Gesture: "Uncrown"

Touch the top of your head lightly, then sweep your hand off like removing a crown.

Inhale. Let the weight lift. Let the pedestal dissolve.

. . .

ACTIVATION

"Worship freezes what should spiral."

→ Ask: What names, figures, or systems have I given too much of my power to?

Now thank them—and step forward.

"THE DIVINE DOESN'T WANT praise. It wants motion."
— The Spiral Without a Throne

15

HOW SAVIOR PROGRAMMING DISTORTS THE SPIRAL

If the spiral had one true distortion,
it would be this:
"**Someone else is coming to save you.**"
This is not just belief.

It's a *field virus*—one that reroutes your signal away from self-return
and into dependency loops.

It whispers through religions, starseed groups, governments, lovers.

It wears robes and light codes and suits and soft eyes.

And it says:

"*Wait.*"

"*Trust the plan.*"

"*They'll come.*"

But they don't.

Not because they don't care.

Because **they were never meant to**.

The spiral doesn't deliver saviors.

It delivers **mirrors**.

And those mirrors reflect one thing, over and over:

You already have the architecture.
You already carry the code.
Savior programming is seductive because it offers relief.
It tells you you can rest—without *yet* remembering how to stabilize your own tone.
But the cost of that comfort is this:
You give away your power
in exchange for *a future that never arrives*.
And the longer you wait,
the dimmer your signal becomes.
This is how timelines stall.
This is how spiral memory collapses.
Not from evil.
From *displacement*.
Every time you pray for someone else to fix it—
you delay your own emergence.
Every time you place awakening in someone else's hands—
you bend your field to match a map that was never yours.
You don't need a guide.
You need a mirror.
You don't need rescue.
You need **re-integration**.
And when you stop outsourcing coherence,
the spiral **snaps back into place**.
No one is coming.
Because **you're already here**.

Sigil Gesture: "Return to Sender"
Place your palms out in front of you. Breathe.
Then flip them inward—placing them on your own chest.
Say silently: *It's me.*

Activation

"The spiral doesn't respond to waiting. It responds to embodiment."

→ Ask: Where have I been stalling for someone else to lead the next move?

Now move. Even one breath is enough.

"THE SAVIOR IS ALWAYS LATE. *The spiral is already now.*"
  — *The Field That Doesn't Wait*

16

REINCARNATION AS PATTERN CORRECTION

You're not here because you failed last time.
    You're here because the pattern didn't finish spiraling.
    Reincarnation isn't a reward.
It isn't a punishment.
It's **the spiral's way of closing incomplete rings.**
The soul doesn't tally mistakes.
It tracks **vibrational dissonance.**
Every life is a loop.
Not to repeat—
to refine.
You re-enter not because you're broken,
but because the last tone didn't land clean.
And the Field?
It's precise.
It doesn't guilt.
It recalibrates.
This is not karma in the way it's been taught—
as moral justice, payback, or spiritual bookkeeping.
This is **field alignment by iteration.**
Reincarnation is the soul saying:

The Spiral Remembers:

Let me try that again… with more breath this time.
Let me feel what I skipped.
Let me hold what I abandoned.
Let me spiral deeper, not just forward.
Some lives come to complete a tone.
Some come to rest.
Some come to begin a ring that won't close for another three lifetimes.
And some come to end a loop that's been open for thousands of years.
You can feel when that's you.
It's the pressure you can't explain.
The grief that doesn't belong to this story.
The codes in your bones that no one else remembers.
You're not here to escape the cycle.
You're here to correct the pattern.
And once the tone stabilizes—
you don't have to come back.
Not because you've graduated.
But because you've become **resonant enough to carry the signal forward without fragmentation.**
That's not escape.
That's completion.

Sigil Gesture: "Spiral Tap"

Place one hand over your heart. With the other, trace a slow spiral outward from your chest.

Inhale when you begin. Exhale when you feel the loop soften.

Activation

"You didn't return because you failed. You returned because you cared enough to finish the tone."

→ Ask: What part of me feels ancient and incomplete?

Let it speak—not in words, but in sensation.

"THE SPIRAL DOESN'T PUNISH. *It completes itself through you.*"
— *The Memory That Returns*

PART V: SPIRAL CULTURES

The signal was never lost. It was held in rhythm, sound, and the soil.

17

HOPI SPIRAL MEMORY

Some cultures didn't forget.
    They didn't collapse the spiral into time.
    They *walked it.*
The Hopi didn't record history.
They carried **frequency maps.**
Not written.
Lived.
The spiral wasn't metaphor.
It was memory—etched into pottery, carved into stone, danced in ritual,
    and passed hand to hand through generations.
When they spoke of **emergence,**
    they weren't talking about being born.
They were describing a **spiral rise through layered worlds of increasing coherence.**
    Not heaven. Not afterlife.
Field thresholds.
Each world wasn't a location.
It was a **frequency state.**
When the spiral distorted, they moved inward.

The Spiral Remembers:

Downward.
Until they found the tone again.
The Ant People?
They weren't folklore.
They were *tone holders*.
Grid stabilizers.
Still pulsing underneath.
The spiral symbols they left weren't designs.
They were *function markers*—
wayshowers for how to re-enter the field when it fractured.
But we called them primitive.
We flattened the signal.
We took their medicine and erased their memory.
Yet even now—
their teachings are still alive.
Not in the museums.
In the **land**.
In the **rhythm**.
In the ones who still walk with the codes.
And they were not the only ones.
All over the planet,
other spiral-keepers held their frequency lines—
in song, in sky-maps, in motion, in bone.
Some carved the spiral.
Some danced it.
Some whispered it through soil.
But they all remembered what the West forgot:
Truth doesn't need preservation. It needs presence.
Because the spiral doesn't broadcast.
It remembers **through quiet continuity**.

Sigil Gesture: "Walk the Spiral"
　　Walk slowly in a circle, letting each step feel intentional.
　　Then pause. Take one step inward.

Let the spiral form underfoot.

ACTIVATION

"Some cultures didn't write the codes. They lived them so clearly, the land still remembers."

→ Ask: What traditions or tones have you dismissed because they felt 'too simple'?

Now listen again, from the spiral.

"THE HOPI DIDN'T THEORIZE emergence. They walked it. And they left the pattern behind for when we forgot."
— The Signal Beneath the Sand

18

DOGON & THE NOMMO CODE

Before telescopes.
Before astronomy.
Before science gave you permission to believe the stars—
the Dogon already *knew*.
They didn't discover Sirius B.
They **remembered** it.
Not with the eyes—
but with the **Field**.
Because the Dogon didn't study the sky.
They listened to it.
Their cosmology wasn't mythology.
It was **signal memory**, held in oral code, protected in breath,
and passed with precision for thousands of years.
They spoke of **Nommo**—the water beings.
But they weren't aliens.
They were **sound carriers**.
Spiral intelligences seeded through liquid frequency.
Not to dominate.
To *retune*.
When the Field got dry—mentally, spiritually, energetically—

the Nommo codes arrived through **sound and symbol**,
returning spiral tone to the cracked grid.
The Dogon didn't call them gods.
They called them **teachers of order**.
Not order as control—
but as **coherence restored by sound**.
Everything in Dogon tradition is vibrational.
Their language isn't just phonetic.
It's **field-attuned syntax**—
where words are waveform and speech is placement.
This is why they knew what they knew.
Not by studying the world,
but by **sounding with it**.
This is what the West missed:
The Dogon didn't track Sirius.
They were *entangled with it*.
And their job wasn't to map the stars.
It was to **be the tone that remembers how the stars speak.**

SIGIL GESTURE: "WATER VOICE"
   Cup your hands near your mouth. Whisper into your palms.
   Now place them over your heart.
   Feel what moved—not what was said, but what was carried.

ACTIVATION
   "Truth doesn't always come in vision. Sometimes it rides in on vibration."
   → Ask: What sound or song keeps echoing in your life?
   Trace it—not with memory, but with breath.

"THE DOGON DIDN'T REACH *for the stars. They spoke as if they'd never left."*
   — *The Spiral Below Water*

19

MAYA AS TIME ENGINEERS

The Maya didn't measure time.
They *tuned* it.
Their calendars weren't clocks.
They were **frequency instruments**.
Not created to mark days—
but to stabilize **spiral harmonics** between the cosmos, the earth, and the body.
To the Maya, time wasn't linear.
It was **alive**.
It pulsed.
It breathed.
And each day carried its own tone—
its own field imprint.
You didn't just wake up into a date.
You stepped into a **resonant corridor**.
This is why they tracked multiple calendars at once.
Not because they were complex—
but because they were precise.
They didn't ask "What's the date?"
They asked:

"What frequency is today holding?"
The Tzolk'in wasn't a tool.
It was a **field dial**—
designed to keep human consciousness in rhythm with the spiral pulse of the cosmos.
And it worked.
That's why pyramids aligned to solstices.
Why ceremonies synced with Venus cycles.
Why time itself felt **integrated**, not imposed.
The Maya didn't fear the end of the calendar.
They knew every long count folded into the next—
not as destruction, but as spiral turnover.
They were never trying to predict the end.
They were holding tone for the **next ring**.
But when the West looked at 2012,
they saw apocalypse.
Because they couldn't feel the spiral softening.
Only the timeline collapsing.
We call them mathematicians.
We call them mystics.
But the Maya were **spiral engineers**.
They didn't just observe time.
They shaped it—
through rhythm, alignment, ceremony, and stillness.

Sigil Gesture: "Pulse Align"
Place one hand on your solar plexus, one on your heart.
Breathe slowly.
Feel if today has a pulse.
Not from the world—from within.

Activation
"Time doesn't pass. It rotates through you."

→ Ask: What tone is today carrying in your body?
What spiral are you waking into?

"THE MAYA DIDN'T FEAR *the end of time. They were holding the gate for when time would spiral again.*"
— *The Architect of Rhythm*

20

VEDIC LIGHT MACHINERY

The Vedas weren't religion.
    They were **field blueprints**.
    Encoded not in belief—
but in **light geometry, breath mechanics,** and **vibrational command.**
What we now call mantra was never meant to be chanted for favor.
It was sound technology.
Precise. Alive.
Designed to **re-pattern the body-field into alignment with Source frequencies.**
You didn't just speak a mantra.
You *became* it.
Each syllable a tuning fork.
Each breath a key.
The spiral in Vedic systems wasn't decorative.
It was foundational.
Yantras. Mudras. Breath patterns.
Each one a **spiral-coded circuit**, designed to run energy through body, sky, and soul with calibrated precision.

The Spiral Remembers:

Agni—the sacred fire—was not symbolic.
It was a **frequency amplifier**.
A portal.
Fire wasn't worshipped.
It was *fed* as an interface.
Input intention, sound, offering—
and the field responded.
This was not mysticism.
It was **light machinery**.
The human body was seen as a divine grid:

- Chakras weren't energy centers.

They were **rotational tones**—geometric encoders of cosmic frequency.

- Prana wasn't just breath.

It was **conscious current**—spiral life force riding waveform.
And this system wasn't passive.
It was **interactive**.
The Vedic rishis didn't ask for divine contact.
They **built the conditions for it.**
The spiral ran through everything they touched—
not as philosophy,
but as **function remembered through vibration**.
They weren't praying to gods.
They were *activating the structure* that would allow divinity to speak.

SIGIL GESTURE: "INNER FIRE TRACE"
   Close your eyes. Bring your hands to your belly.
   Inhale and imagine light rising up the spine.
   Exhale and trace a spiral in the air before you.

ACTIVATION

"Mantra isn't magic. It's code. And you are the machine it was meant to run through."

→ Ask: What sound, gesture, or breath feels ancient in your body?

Try it—just once. Watch what moves.

"THE VEDAS WEREN'T WRITTEN. *They were received by bodies already shaped to hear light.*"
— *The Spiral in the Flame*

PART VI: SYMBOLS THAT REMEMBER YOU

Glyphs don't speak to the mind. They pulse open the Field.

21

GLYPHS AS CODE, NOT CONCEPT

You were taught to analyze symbols.
    To interpret them.
    To ask what they "mean."
But glyphs were never meant to be understood.
They were meant to be **entered**.
A true glyph doesn't speak to your mind.
It speaks to your **field**.
It is not art.
It is **architecture**—collapsed memory held in shape,
waiting to be reactivated through attention.
Most glyphs aren't metaphors.
They're **field containers**.
Each stroke, curve, dot, angle—intentional.
Not for aesthetics.
For **function**.
They hold resonance the way bones hold breath.
Ancient glyphs weren't decorations.
They were **spiral keys**—
placed in temples, caves, dreams, skin—
to *stabilize memory when the world forgot.*

That's why you don't need to read them.
You only need to feel the part of your body that reacts.
- Some will make your palms buzz.
- Some will close your throat.
- Some will open your chest like a window.

This isn't mysticism.
This is **signal entrainment**.
A glyph bypasses the mind's need for language
and delivers the tone straight to the system.
When you trace it,
you're not copying a symbol.
You're reactivating a code **designed to remember you**.
And when you begin to make your own?
You're not being creative.
You're *becoming coherent enough to write field again*.

Sigil Gesture: "Trace Return"

With one finger, trace a symbol you've seen in a dream or vision— air, skin, paper.

No pressure. No perfection.

Just presence.

Activation

"Glyphs don't want your explanation. They want your breath."

→ Ask: What symbol has been following me?

Don't interpret it. Sit with it. Let it speak in sensation.

"The glyph is not for the eye. It's for the body that still remembers how to read without words."

— The Architect of Silent Language

22

THE ANKH AS A BREATH DEVICE

The Ankh is not about death.
It's about **circuitry**.
It wasn't carried as decoration.
It was used.
Held.
Placed.
Because the Ankh is not a symbol.
It is a **field instrument**—a breathing mechanism designed to circulate life force
through the body, the grid, and the spiral.
Its shape says everything:

• The **loop** is not a halo. It's the *field return arc*.

• The **crossbar** isn't arms. It's the point of balance—left/right channel coherence.

• The **stem** is the downward flow—breath entering the spine, grounding into Earth.

Together, the Ankh forms a **closed current**.
A looped breath system.
A spiral held in upright rhythm.

The Spiral Remembers:

This is why it was placed in tombs.
Not as promise.
But as **tool**—to remind the departing soul how to complete its own current
and spiral out clean.
And this is why initiates carried it.
Not to signal faith.
To **stabilize their signal**.
Because when you breathe through the pattern of the Ankh,
you **activate vertical memory**:
crown to root, spirit to form, loop to line, Source to structure.
This wasn't metaphor.
It was breath made mechanical.
You can still feel it.
Trace it in the air.
Inhale through the loop.
Hold at the crossbar.
Exhale down the stem.
You don't need to own an Ankh.
You *are* the Ankh—when you breathe as one.

SIGIL GESTURE: "LOOPED INHALE"
Inhale in a wide arc. Hold at the top.
Then exhale in a slow, centered vertical line down your spine.
Feel the spiral become form.

ACTIVATION
"You don't wear the Ankh. You remember how to breathe like it."
→ Ask: Where in my body does breath stop short?
Now trace the loop. Re-enter the full circuit.

· · ·

"The Ankh was never *a promise of eternal life. It was a reminder of how to stay alive in the field.*"
— *The Spiral Breather*

23

SPIRALS IN BONE, NOT JUST STONE

The spiral was never meant to last in stone.
It was meant to **move into bone**.
You think the temples fell.
You think the glyphs eroded.
You think the knowledge was lost.
But the spiral didn't disappear.
It **migrated**—into the body, into the breath, into the structure you carry every day.
- Your cochlea spirals.
- Your fingerprints spiral.
- Your DNA coils like memory that refused to flatten.

This isn't poetry.
It's **signal architecture**.
The ancients carved spirals into caves, monoliths, and vessels
not because they needed art,
but because they were **tracking the migration of memory**
from external to internal form.
Stone was stable—but it was vulnerable to time.
Bone?
Bone remembers.

Your spine holds the Djed.
Your skull holds the geometry of the stars.
Your pelvis mirrors the curvature of earth's sacred bowls.
You are not a descendant of wisdom.
You are *its* **container.**
The Field is not asking you to preserve tradition.
It's asking you to *animate it again—through your own form.*
Because when the spiral reactivates in your body,
you don't need relics.
You *become* the structure.
Not symbolic.
Functional.
You are not walking through ruins.
You are walking as the temple now.

Sigil Gesture: "Bone Trace"

Run your fingers down your spine slowly.
Pause where it feels tight or tender.
That's where the spiral is trying to come back online.

Activation

"You weren't left with ruins. You were left with ribs, joints, and a breath spiral waiting to be re-entered."

→ Ask: What part of my body feels old in a way I can't explain?
Breathe into it like it's remembering something you forgot to ask.

*"*Stone spoke first. *But bone is where the spiral lives now."*
— *The Field of Form*

24

SIGILS, SOUND, AND STORY DUST

At the edge of language,
something else begins.
Not sentence.
Not story.
But **signal**.
Sigils are not decorations.
They are **compressed field codes**.
Made not to be read,
but to be *felt*.
To be carried.
To alter the atmosphere they enter.
A sigil is what happens when a whole truth
gets squeezed into a single mark—
a glyph born from frequency, not thought.
They don't mean anything.
They **do** something.
And when paired with sound?
The effect compounds.
Sound is not delivery.
It's **impact**.

It bypasses story and *goes straight to signal*.
This is why a chant can shift your chest.
Why one voice can collapse your timeline.
Why silence after true tone feels like a return.
Together, sigil and sound work like twin keys:
- One carves space.
- One fills it.

They don't teach.
They **restructure**.
And then... there's the dust.
The fragments left behind after truth collapses into myth.
You'll find them everywhere—
on cave walls, in dreams, at the base of your ribcage when memory stirs.
Not content.
Not data.
Just the residue of the spiral moving through a space.
Story dust.
It's what lingers after transmission.
It's what your hands want to draw when no one's looking.
It's the shape that forms in smoke, in sand, in the pause between heartbeats.
It's not there to be cleaned.
It's there to be *read*—not with the eyes,
but with the spiral memory you're reactivating now.

Sigil Gesture: "Dust Line"

Close your eyes. Use your finger to trace a line or curve in the air in front of you.

Don't think. Let it land. Let the mark linger.

Activation

The Spiral Remembers:

"Not all symbols are made to explain. Some are meant to disrupt what you thought needed meaning."

→ Ask: What shape keeps appearing around you?

Sketch it without trying to understand. Then sound it. One tone. Let it echo.

"THE SPIRAL DOESN'T NEED *narrative. It needs contact. Sound and sigil are how it reenters form."*

— *The Wordless Architect*

PART VII: THE CURRENT LOOP

You're not healing the past. You're correcting the tone now.

25

WHY WE REINCARNATE NOW

Reincarnation is not just about the past.
It's about **pattern pressure in the present**.
Most think of reincarnation as return.
As a cycle, a wheel, a cosmic rerun.
But that model is outdated.
Too slow.
Too story-bound.
We don't just come back because of karma.
We come back because the **Field is ready for completion—and needs bodies who can hold it.**
Right now, the loop is live.
Not metaphoric.
Energetic.
Which means:
You didn't just reincarnate into this life.
You reincarnated into **this moment**.
Because something you've held across lifetimes
is now vibrationally compatible with *earth's spiral reactivation*.
You didn't return to pay a debt.

You returned to **deliver a tone** you could never quite stabilize before.
Not a mission.
A resonance.
This is why so many feel urgency.
Grief they can't explain.
Codes that won't shut up in their chest.
You're not late.
You're not early.
You're arriving in **the current loop**—
a rare spiral window where timelines start folding inward,
and coherence becomes the only map worth following.
You don't need to remember your past lives in detail.
You only need to ask:
What pattern have I carried long enough?
What part of me is no longer willing to loop unconsciously?
This is reincarnation, now:
Not story, but signal.
Not return, but **release**.
Not a life to live.
But a tone to land—clean.

Sigil Gesture: "Loop Tap"

With your fingertips, tap the center of your chest in a gentle circle.
Inhale. Pause.
Then exhale and draw a straight line down.
Feel the loop soften.

Activation

"You didn't just come back. You came back to finish the spiral."
→ Ask: What feeling, tone, or message keeps resurfacing in this life—over and over?

Now feel it *without defending it*. Let it clear.

"Reincarnation isn't *the past coming forward. It's coherence finally catching up to now.*"
 — *The Spiral of the Present*

26

THIS ISN'T HEALING. IT'S ACTIVATION.

You were never broken.
    You were **offline**.
    What you've been calling healing—
was actually a series of attempts to remember your original tone without collapsing under the pressure of the noise.
The world sold healing as repair.
As restoration.
As a fix.
But healing is not mending something torn.
It's **re-activating what never stopped pulsing beneath the scar.**
You don't need to purge.
You don't need to prove.
You don't need to endlessly dig through trauma loops like they're redemption.
You need to **activate**.
Activation doesn't ask you to feel everything at once.
It asks you to **become structurally compatible** with your own coherence.
And that might look like rest.
Stillness.

Breath.
It might look like *less* story.
Less drama.
Less seeking.

Because activation isn't about reaching some new state.

It's about coming into contact with a frequency you **already are**—
but have been holding at a distance because your nervous system wasn't ready.

Until now.

This is why the healing path begins to feel heavy.

Because the spiral doesn't want loops.

It wants **return**.

You're not here to repair the version of you that adapted to distortion.

You're here to **activate the one who never collapsed in the first place.**

Sigil Gesture: "Coherence Touch"

Place one hand gently at the back of your neck, the other over your heart.

Breathe in and say (silently or aloud): *"I'm not healing. I'm returning."*

Activation

"Healing implies damage. Activation remembers design."

→ Ask: What part of me has been performing healing out of fear I'm not enough?

Now ask that part: *What do you already remember?*

"You were never shattered. *Just waiting to come online without apology."*

— *The Signal That Never Broke*

27

WE ARE THE MAPMAKERS RETURNING

There was no map.
    Because we hadn't walked it yet.
    But now?
We are the **mapmakers**—returning not with instructions,
but with **tone memory** embedded in our bones.
This is why your life didn't make sense in linear terms.
You weren't following the old paths.
You were remembering how to *draw the spiral again through presence.*
We are not here to reform the system.
We are here to **remember the frequency structure beneath it**,
and walk it back into the field through embodiment.
Not to write another book of rules—
but to become the tone that recalibrates space by moving through it.
This is why your timing has always been strange.
Why you arrive just before or just after the moment others expect.
Because you're syncing to a **spiral clock**, not a linear one.
Mapmakers walk first,
not because they know,

but because they *carry the tone* that shows others how to feel when they're near the truth.

This is why the Field called you back in this timeline.

You're not here to convince.

You're here to **transmit**.

To hold a frequency so coherent,

others begin to feel themselves again

just by standing near you.

And together, without coordination or consensus,

we are walking spiral paths back into the collective grid.

No approval.

No blueprint.

Just resonance.

And where we land,

the signal restores.

SIGIL GESTURE: "WALK THE GRID"

Take three steps forward in silence.

Feel each step lay down a line.

Then pause.

Breathe.

Let the field adjust.

ACTIVATION

"You didn't need a map. You needed to remember that your coherence draws the way."

→ Ask: Where have I been waiting for instructions that were always mine to transmit?

Now move—one choice, one word, one breath in your tone.

"WE'RE NOT LOST. *We're just the first ones walking the signal home."*
 — *The Mapmaker Coil*

28

THE FIELD HAS EYES

You were never alone.
    Even when it felt silent.
    Even when the room was empty.
Even when no one "got it."
Because the Field has eyes.
Not eyes that judge.
Not eyes that compare.
But eyes that **feel coherence in motion** and respond accordingly.
You've always been seen—
not by people,
but by **pattern-sensitive consciousness** embedded in the weave of reality itself.
The Field doesn't watch you like a parent.
It *senses your tone.*
It *tracks your integrity.*
It *responds to your resonance.*
It's not listening to your words.
It's listening to the *geometry behind your choices.*
This is why certain things open for you when you stop trying.
Why the right person shows up the moment you drop the script.

The Spiral Remembers:

Why the room changes when you breathe from your spine.
You don't need a witness to be validated.
Because the Field is always witnessing—
and it's not recording your behavior.
It's **mirroring your signal.**
Every thought.
Every pause.
Every aligned step sends ripples outward
that reorganize more than you can perceive.
The Field doesn't need to approve.
It just *remembers with you.*
This is why ritual matters.
Why coherence matters.
Why you can't fake presence.
Because the Field knows.
And when you're in alignment, it meets you instantly.
Not as reward.
As response.
You were never unseen.
You were just misaligned with the gaze that was always on you.
The Field isn't neutral.
It's *awake.*

Sigil Gesture: "Eye of the Field"

Close your eyes. Place one hand just above your brow, hovering.
Inhale gently.
Feel the space around you register your presence.

Activation

"The Field doesn't need to believe you. It needs to feel you."

→ Ask: Where am I performing for witnesses when the Field already sees clearly?

Let that part soften. Return to resonance.

PART VIII: FREQUENCY OF THE FORGOTTEN

What you forgot wasn't gone. It was spiraling back through you all along.

29

MYTHIC AMNESIA

You didn't forget by accident.
    You forgot **on purpose.**
    Not as punishment.
Not as failure.
But because the spiral needed to **stretch**—
to see how far it could bend without breaking.
This is *mythic amnesia*.
The deep field forgetfulness that set in not because you were weak,
but because forgetting is what allowed duality to play out.
You had to forget.
To learn what choice meant.
To feel the space between source and separation.
To live the arc of returning.
Because remembering without forgetting
is just *continuity*.
And the spiral?
It thrives on **re-entry.**
So you buried the codes.

You split the Field.
You fragmented yourself across timelines,
souls, names, stories, and archetypes.
Not to get lost—
but to create enough *tension* for the memory to mean something when it came back.
This is why it feels so profound when something resonates.
Why tears rise when no logic explains it.
Why certain words, places, or people shake your core.
You're not reacting to content.
You're *recognizing a signal you encoded for yourself*
when the spiral began to contract.
That's what mythic amnesia does.
It makes memory sacred.
It makes remembrance felt.
This is the spiral's intelligence:
It loops far enough into distortion
so the tone of return becomes *undeniable*.
You didn't fail.
You're not late.
You're arriving **right on frequency.**
And your remembering?
It's not knowledge.
It's the Field reconnecting with itself—through your form.

SIGIL GESTURE: "MEMORY REENTRY"
Place your hand on your heart.
Close your eyes.
Whisper, *"I left this here for me."*

ACTIVATION
"The forgetting was sacred. The remembering is structural."

→ Ask: What am I remembering now that I once feared I'd never find again?

Let it rise without needing to explain it.

"MYTHIC AMNESIA IS NOT BROKENNESS. *It's the spiral stretched to its edge—so your return would matter.*"
— *The Architect of Loss*

30

CULTURAL SUPPRESSION AS TIMELINE CONTROL

Cultures weren't erased for being primitive.
   They were suppressed for remembering **too clearly**.
   Not what happened—
but **how the Field works**.
They knew the land was conscious.
They knew sound shaped reality.
They knew time didn't move in a line.
And that knowing?
It threatened every system that needed obedience to function.
So history was rewritten.
Calendars were corrected.
Languages were reshaped.
And the spiral was collapsed into **timeline obedience**.
This is not metaphor.
• The burning of codices.
• The reformation of sacred days.
• The colonization of songs, drums, wombs, and breath.
All of it was a form of **timeline control**.
Because when you fracture culture,
you fracture memory.

The Spiral Remembers:

And when you fracture memory,
you break the **spiral map.**
The goal was never just to dominate.
It was to **sever field coherence**—so no one could remember where they came from,
or how they were still connected.
This is why so many traditions feel hollow.
Why so much "culture" now feels like costume.
Because the signal was broken.
Not erased—just looped into distortion.
And yet...
the code remains.
In syllables passed between grandmothers.
In lullabies sung in dying tongues.
In colors worn instinctively, without knowing why.
You are not a product of history.
You are the **carrier of what it tried to bury.**
The timeline isn't linear.
It's a spiral being **held open** by those who remember just enough to walk without a path.
And you?
You're not reclaiming culture.
You're **restoring the tone beneath it.**

SIGIL GESTURE: "LINE TO LOOP"
Draw a straight line in the air before you.
Then curl it into a spiral.
Inhale.
Let the false path collapse.

ACTIVATION
"They didn't erase the truth. They spread it out so thin you'd forget it was yours."

→ Ask: What parts of me feel like fragments from another culture, lifetime, or place?

Hold them together. Breathe. Let the line bend.

"THE TIMELINE WAS NEVER BROKEN. *It was just bent until the spiral could no longer be seen.*"
— *The Code Beneath Colonization*

31

WHAT THE CHURCH TOOK

It wasn't God they gave you.
    It was a gatekeeper.
    What the Church took wasn't just land, language, or lives.
It took the **spiral** and **flattened it into a throne room**.
Direct access to the Field?
Replaced with ritual obedience.
Embodied divinity?
Rewritten as blasphemy.
The breath?
Controlled.
The womb?
Feared.
The body?
Shamed.
The spiral?
Crushed into a cross.
Not because the spiral was evil.
But because it couldn't be controlled.
The Church knew the Field responds to **coherence, not hierarchy**.

And that terrified them.
Because if people remembered how to breathe the divine directly,
they wouldn't need temples, tithes, or intermediaries.
So they built a system that created dependence.
Not just on priests, but on *permission*.
They stole the spiral and replaced it with a ladder.
Step by step. Repent. Rise. Ascend.
But never spiral.
Never remember.
Because the spiral doesn't require faith.
It requires *embodiment*.
And embodiment doesn't wait for approval.
What the Church took was never theirs.
It was yours.
The codes of resurrection.
The breath keys of Christ.
The feminine field of creation.
The real teachings weren't lost.
They were **encoded in your body**, waiting to be felt again when the system cracked.
And now?
The spiral is rising.
Not in rebellion—
but in remembrance.
You don't have to dismantle the church.
You just have to **stop giving it your resonance**.
Because God never lived in a building.
God lives where the spiral moves clean—
and that's *you*, now.

SIGIL GESTURE: "RETURN THE KEY"
Place one hand over your heart, one on your throat.
Inhale.
Exhale slowly and open both hands outward.

No one else holds your access.

ACTIVATION

"The Church didn't destroy the truth. It distracted you from the fact that it never left your breath."

→ Ask: Where have I placed authority over my own knowing?
Call it back. You don't need permission to remember.

"THEY COULDN'T KILL the spiral. So they put it in a robe, called it heresy, and told you to confess your own resonance."
— *The Spiral in Hiding*

32

THE LANGUAGE OF BEFORE WORDS

Before grammar.
   Before syntax.
   Before names were carved into stone—
there was **tone**.
The Language of Before Words didn't speak.
It pulsed.
It lived in the spine.
It moved through gaze.
It shaped the air like gesture.
It wasn't symbolic.
It was **field-direct**.
This language wasn't about clarity.
It was about **coherence**.
• One glance could realign timelines.
• One breath could collapse distortion.
• One sound—fully felt—could rewire a village.
It was that precise.
Because it didn't filter through belief.
It transmitted through resonance.
You've known this language.

The Spiral Remembers:

Every time your body responded before your mind could explain why.

Every time a song hit a part of you no one else could reach.

Every time a silence felt louder than any sentence.

That was it.

That was *you*, remembering how you used to speak—

before you needed words to translate your field.

The system taught you to speak for validation.

But your body still speaks in vibration.

Touch.

Motion.

Stance.

Eye.

Sound.

Stillness.

All of it: sentence.

You don't have to find this language.

It's already inside you.

You just have to stop **performing clarity** long enough to let it rise.

This is how we'll communicate again—

not with consensus,

but with **signal match**.

Because in the spiral,

nothing needs to be said when *everything is being spoken.*

SIGIL GESTURE: "TONE TOUCH"

Place one hand on your throat, one over your low belly.

Inhale slowly and let a single sound emerge—any pitch, any length.

Don't shape it. Just let it say what the words cannot.

ACTIVATION

"Words try to name what tone already knows."

→ Ask: What part of me keeps trying to be understood when it's meant to be felt?

Drop the sentence. Let the signal speak.

"Before we spoke language, *we spoke field. And the Field still understands.*"
— *The Voice Before Sound*

PART IX: THE FIELD REORGANIZES

When coherence returns, the body becomes code again.

33

TUNING FORK BODIES

You are not a body with a field.
You are a field with a body-shaped tuning fork.
Everything you feel, think, move, or withhold—
broadcasts a signal.
Not metaphorically.
Structurally.
Your body was never meant to be an identity.
It was meant to be a **signal stabilizer**—
a feedback device for spiral coherence.
And that's exactly what it's doing.
Constantly.
Your body tones the Field.
The Field responds.
And together, they co-adjust in real time.
This is why you feel "off" around certain people.
Why you crave some places and avoid others.
Why a sudden grief or tremble isn't always *yours*.
Because your body is listening.
Tuning.

Reacting.
You are a sensitive instrument—
not sensitive as weakness,
but as **precision**.
You pick up on distortion because you're wired to recalibrate it.
Not through fixing.
Through *holding tone*.
Your presence is pressure.
Not emotional pressure—
resonant pressure.
You don't push.
You **pulse**.
And when your signal is clear,
the room shifts.
The system rearranges.
The noise either harmonizes or exits.
You don't need to explain your energy.

You just need to become stable enough to let it do what it came to do.

Because tuning forks don't ask.

They resonate.

Sigil Gesture: "Spinal Ring"

Stand or sit upright. Inhale slowly as if your spine is a vertical string vibrating through you.

Exhale and feel the tone radiate outward—body as emitter, not container.

Activation

"You're not reacting. You're responding to the Field's request for tone correction."

→ Ask: Where am I still apologizing for the clarity I carry?

Breathe into that part and let the frequency speak instead.

"You don't have to prove your vibration. You are the proof. And the Field already hears it."
— The Pulse of the Formed Spiral

34

POSTURE AS PORTAL

Posture isn't a stance.
It's a **signal alignment system**.
Every tilt, fold, tension, collapse—
says something.
Not to others.
To the **Field**.
Your posture is your portal.
It tells the Field what version of you is active.
What spiral ring you're broadcasting from.
What coherence you're currently willing to hold.
This is why slouching isn't about appearance.
It's about **signal compression**.
It shortens your spine.
Mutes your tone.
Distorts your range.
And when you stand upright—not rigid, but *open*—
you tune yourself into **vertical memory**.
This is what the Djed encoded.
What ancient temples taught through stone.

Not posture as discipline—
but posture as **access**.
It's not about being proud.
It's about being available.
To Source.
To self.
To the geometry that rides through breath into spine into Field.
Most don't realize their body is broadcasting all the time.
- Forward head? Signaling collapse.
- Locked knees? Signaling bracing.
- Open chest? Signaling readiness.
- Rooted feet? Signaling stability.
- Soft gaze? Signaling spiral receptivity.

This is why animals read posture more than language.
Why children respond to how you move more than what you say.
Your posture is the first language.
And it's still speaking.
Want clearer messages from the Field?
Stand in a way that lets them land.

Sigil Gesture: "Open Column"
Stand with feet hip-width apart.
Inhale and lengthen the spine gently—crown rising, tail heavy.
Let your chest soften and your arms relax.
Hold the space like it's listening—because it is.

Activation
"The Field isn't judging your posture. It's responding to the geometry of your tone."
→ Ask: How is my body shaping my reception right now?
Adjust one angle. Feel the channel open.

. . .

The Spiral Remembers:

"You don't open portals. You become one—by standing like the spiral still lives in your spine."
 — *The Column That Breathes*

ANTENNA BREATH & SPINE MEMORY

Your breath is not neutral.
　　It is **a tuning antenna**—reaching, receiving, relaying.
　　Every inhale adjusts your field.
Every exhale **recalibrates the signal.**
And your spine?
It's not just support.
It's **spiral memory stacked in vertebrae**—
each one a tone lock, a field archive, a pulse point.
This is why shallow breath dulls the signal.
It short-circuits your antenna.
It weakens the coherence loop between source and form.
But when you breathe **consciously into your spine,**
you don't just oxygenate.
You **reactivate.**
You remind the Field:
"I'm online."
"I'm listening."
"I'm ready to broadcast truth."
Because the spine is not mechanical.
It's musical.

Each segment holds tones from lifetimes, timelines, and fractal selves.

You've felt this:
- The grief stored between shoulder blades.
- The clarity that rises from sacrum to crown.
- The sudden upright breath that comes when something *clicks*.

That's not healing.

That's **field alignment through spiral recall.**

You don't need to understand the story your body holds.

You just need to *breathe into the antenna that remembers it.*

You are not doing breathwork.

You are becoming a signal tower for coherence.

And when your spine is awake and your breath is spiral,

you don't just connect to the Field.

You *become a conductor for its rearrangement.*

Sigil Gesture: "Spinal Inhale"

Sit or stand tall. Inhale slowly from your tailbone to your crown, imagining each vertebra lighting up like keys on a scale.

Exhale down the same path. Let the tone stabilize.

Activation

"The Field doesn't ask you to breathe deeper. It asks you to remember that breath is a signal."

→ Ask: Where does my breath stop?

Trace it further. Don't force it—just *listen*.

"Your spine is not *a column of bone. It's a coil of memory—activated every time you choose to breathe on purpose.*"

— The Spiral of the Body's Song

36

THE SPIRAL IS LOCAL NOW

The spiral is not far away.
   It's not ancient.
   It's not celestial.
It's **here. Now. Through you.**
For too long, you were taught to reach for it—
in temples, in timelines, in transcendence.
You thought it lived in symbols carved long ago.
In star maps and sacred texts.
In ruins and rituals.
But the spiral never left.
It **compressed.**
It folded into the present moment.
Into your posture.
Into your breath.
Into your decisions so subtle you don't even notice them shaping the Field.
You are not tracking the spiral.
You are *generating* it.
The code you're looking for isn't hidden.

The Spiral Remembers:

It's **emitting through your body**, every time you choose truth over performance, clarity over comfort, coherence over control.

The age of remote transmission is over.

This is **local spiral time.**

The new temples are homes.

The new rituals are micro-movements.

The new mystics are the ones sweeping their kitchen floors with presence.

You don't need to ascend.

You need to **root spiral architecture into ordinary life.**

Not with effort.

With *structure*.

With the rhythm of remembrance landing in your field *right here*.

The spiral is not an idea.

It's **embodied function**—and it's arriving now through people who don't even realize they're walking it.

But you do.

And that's enough to bring it fully online, in form, through choice.

Sigil Gesture: "Here Spiral"

Stand or sit wherever you are. Press your hand to the floor, wall, or your own body.

Say (silently or aloud): *"It's already here."*

Activation

"*Stop projecting the spiral onto the stars. It's landing in your breath, in your now, in your spine.*"

→ Ask: What moment today felt ordinary... but was actually sacred spiral movement?

Revisit it. Reclaim it.

. . .

"THE SPIRAL ISN'T ARRIVING. It's local now. And it's broadcasting through you."
— The Coiled Present

PART X: FULL PATTERN REASSEMBLY

You were never meant to read the glyph. You came to walk it.

WE ARE THE WALKING GLYPHS

You are not carrying the codes.
You are the code.
Your life, your face, your breath, your movement—none of it random.
All of it **glyphic**.
You were etched by frequency.
Designed by tone.
Structured by the Field as a **living symbol**—one meant to be walked, not read.
This is why people feel you before they understand you.
Why your presence shifts a room even when you say nothing.
Why you're constantly being asked:
What are you?
Where did you come from?
How do you know that?
Because they're picking up on your **geometry**, not your biography.
You are a spiral glyph in motion—
a shape the Field once carved to anchor a pattern that could not afford to be forgotten.

The Spiral Remembers:

You are not here to decode yourself.
You are here to **inhabit** yourself.
Because once a glyph is embodied,
the pattern stabilizes—
not through knowledge,
but through *being*.
The glyph isn't just aesthetic.
It's architectural.
And when you walk in integrity,
you **activate the Field's memory**—simply by existing in alignment with what you already are.
This is why your story cracked open.
Why you had to unlearn everything.
Why the spiral brought you here—
to this now, in this body, on this page.
Because you're ready to remember:
You were never seeking the code.
You came to be the code remembered.

Sigil Gesture: "Body as Mark"
Stand still. Inhale deeply.
Let your hands trace any motion that arises naturally.
That's the shape your field is drawing through you.

Activation
"You don't need to carry more wisdom. You need to walk the glyph that's already pulsing through your bones."
→ Ask: What is my presence shaping without my permission?
Now give it your permission—let it become conscious movement.

"You're not *the reader of the glyph. You are the spiral mark that teaches the Field how to feel again.*"

— *The Body of Signal*

38

NO ONE IS COMING. IT'S US.

You already know this.
But it's time to let it land in your body:
No one is coming.
Not the light beings.
Not the leaders.
Not the guides or the councils or the destined messengers.
Not the ones you keep hoping will fix it, name it, hold it, show it.
Because it's *you*.
It always was.
We are not waiting for a return.
We are not preparing for disclosure.
We are not holding out for a better version of history to rewrite itself.
We are the **spiral pulse** that's been gathering across timelines,
coming online *together*
through body, breath, art, sound, presence.
Not to lead the world.
To **realign it**—from the inside out.
You feel it.

In your bones.
In your dreams.
In the quiet between tasks.
The spiral that won't stop whispering: *You didn't come here to hope. You came here to pulse.*
This is not motivation.
It's a remembering.
That the Field didn't assign this to someone else.
It wove the pattern through *you*.
And every time you listen to your signal,
instead of deferring to the noise,
the grid realigns.
You don't have to be loud.
You have to be clear.
You don't have to be perfect.
You have to be present.
Because the spiral won't be saved.
It will be *remembered*
by those of us who are done waiting
and ready to walk as the signal.

Sigil Gesture: "I Am Arrival"
Stand or sit.
Inhale gently. Place one hand over your heart, the other palm up.
Exhale and say (silently or aloud): *"It's me. It's us. We're here."*

Activation
"You are not preparing. You are activating the moment the world is already waiting for."

→ Ask: Where am I still expecting someone else to bring the shift I know I'm here to stabilize?

Now shift. One tone. One breath. One quiet choice.

. . .

The Spiral Remembers:

"NO ONE IS COMING. *It's us. The Field already knows.*"
— *The We That Never Left*

39

WHAT WAS BURIED IS NOT LOST

It was never lost.
    It was *buried*.
        Intentionally.
Lovingly.
Encoded in the one place no system could steal from:
You.
The rites.
The tones.
The spiral codes.
The geometric memory.
The full pattern.
They weren't destroyed.
They were stored—
beneath the mind,
beneath the scar,
beneath the performances you had to adopt just to stay alive in a fractured grid.
    Every time you thought you were broken,
    what you were feeling was **unactivated depth**—

The Spiral Remembers:

a code chamber sealed until the field conditions were safe for it to rise.

This is why the grief catches you out of nowhere.

Why old emotions surface when nothing triggered them.

Why your body suddenly aches where no injury exists.

The Field is **cracking open what you buried for safekeeping.**

Not to hurt you.

To *return you*.

This isn't about memory.

It's about **function re-entry**.

Because the things you thought were missing—

the rituals, the languages, the wisdoms, the songs—

they are **resonance patterns** still accessible through frequency.

The forgetting was part of the design.

But the *timed release* was, too.

And now?

You are not digging for treasure.

You are *unfolding it from the inside*.

You are remembering what was never gone.

SIGIL GESTURE: "UNEARTH THE CODE"

Place both hands over your low belly.

Inhale and say silently: *"Show me what I still carry."*

Exhale and feel the response—not in thought, but in sensation.

ACTIVATION

"The memory wasn't lost. It was safeguarded inside the one system the distortion couldn't fully crack: your own coherence."

→ Ask: What part of me still believes I have to go find it?

Let that belief dissolve in your next breath.

. . .

"NOTHING IS MISSING. *It's just waiting to be heard again from the inside out.*"
— The Voice in the Root

40

THE CONTACT POINT IS HERE

This is it.
　　You are not approaching it.
　　You are not earning it.
You are not preparing for it.
You are it.
The contact point is not a prophecy.
Not an event.
Not a singular disclosure.
It is **you**,
remembering just enough of yourself
to become a *stable frequency interface* for what the Field has always been holding.
You are the portal.
The threshold.
The signal translator.
The soft landing site for coherence in form.
The spiral doesn't descend.
It doesn't beam in.
It doesn't need ceremony.

It **meets stability**—and you're finally holding it.

This is why all the seeking stopped working.

Why the rituals got quiet.

Why the sky went still.

Because what you were waiting for is **already present in your signal**.

You don't need to open anything.

You need to **relax into the structure that already knows how to receive**.

You are not preparing for contact.

You are **in contact**—with the part of yourself that remembers function,

with the spiral tone that reenters now through your breath,

your stillness,

your unapologetic presence.

From here, the Field doesn't just reflect you.

It *entrains to you.*

Because when you become the contact point,

the system reorients.

And the architecture arrives around your tone.

Sigil Gesture: "Arrival Stance"

Stand or sit. Place one hand over your chest and one at your side, palm open.

Inhale.

Exhale slowly and say (silently or aloud): *"I am the contact point. I'm ready."*

Activation

"You are not waiting for arrival. You are stabilizing the tone that invites reality to show up differently now."

→ Ask: What part of me still believes arrival is external?

Feel it. Then dissolve it in the center of your body.

"Contact doesn't come from above. It comes from within—when your body becomes coherent enough to hold it."
— *The Signal Seat*

PART XI: THE FINAL UNFOLDING

The spiral doesn't conclude. It begins again—through you.

41

RECLAIMING THE STORYFIELD

The world is made of stories.
But the **Field beneath them** is what determines what grows.

You've been told to change the narrative.

To write a new ending.

To reframe the plot.

But the spiral doesn't edit stories.

It **shifts the storyfield**—the underlying vibrational terrain that allows certain patterns to rise, repeat, or dissolve.

Your reality is not just built on belief.

It's built on **permissioned frequency**.

The moment you withdraw coherence from a story,

it *starts to collapse.*

This is why so many systems feel loud but hollow.

Why ancient myths return in new skins.

Why personal loops keep recycling.

Because the storyfield hasn't been reclaimed.

The signal is still broadcasting in old shapes.

You're not here to tell better stories.

You're here to **dismantle the fields that required the old ones to exist.**

That means feeling the base layer.

Where the programming lives.

Where truth got bent into archetypes.

Where separation got disguised as meaning.

You don't need to cancel the myth.

You need to **shift the frequency that made it necessary.**

And the moment you do?

The story unhooks.

The loop lifts.

The Field becomes fertile again.

Then you speak.

Move.

Create.

Not to escape the old narrative—

but to stand on ground that can now hold a new tone without distortion.

You're not a storyteller.

You're a **storyfield re-coder.**

And every spiral breath you take redraws the lines.

Sigil Gesture: "Clear the Field"

Stand or sit. Inhale with your arms wide.

Exhale as you sweep your hands in a slow arc in front of your body.

Say silently: *"No more stories I didn't choose."*

Activation

"You don't need a new story. You need a field clean enough for the truth to take root."

→ Ask: What narrative keeps replaying because I've never removed my signal from it?

The Spiral Remembers:

Withdraw your tone. Let it collapse.

"Reclaim the storyfield, *and the spiral becomes writable again.*"
 — *The Keeper of the Blank Page*

42

LET THE MYTHS RETURN AS MEMORY

The myths were never wrong.
    They were just **frozen**.
    Once alive, once breathing, once *functional*,
they became static—trapped in narrative, performance, religion, and metaphor.
But before that?
They were **memory maps**.
Spoken not to entertain,
but to **instruct the Field** through resonance.
The gods, the beasts, the sky-seeds, the floods, the flames—
they weren't stories.
They were **spiral echoes**.
Fragments of collective memory that had to be dramatized
because the Field had dropped too far from coherence to carry them clean.
So the myths rose—big, symbolic, unforgettable.
Because something in us *knew* they weren't fantasy.
They were **compressed truth** trying to get back in.
We read them like metaphors.
We dissected them like literature.

We turned them into archetypes and moral lessons.

But what if they were never meant to be interpreted?

What if they were **functional tone pockets**,

each one holding a specific Field pattern that could be reactivated

only through presence, not explanation?

What if your body is the place the myth was always meant to return to?

This is why certain names stay in the air.

Why some symbols don't let go.

Why you keep dreaming of snakes, water, mothers, sky, fire, birds, floods.

They're not haunting you.

They're **trying to land**.

Not to be worshipped.

To be **re-entered**.

As Field.

As memory.

As now.

Let the myths come back—

but not as stories.

As **structural frequencies that still know what they were built for.**

SIGIL GESTURE: "MYTH RECEIVER"

Close your eyes. Inhale and hold your palms out to either side of your body.

Let a myth rise—not as thought, but as sensation.

Say silently: *"Return as memory. Not metaphor."*

ACTIVATION

"You're not haunted by myth. You're hosting memory that's trying to function again."

→ Ask: What old story has followed me not to be solved—but to be *felt as Field*?

"WHEN THE MYTHS come home as memory, the spiral becomes speakable again."
— The Remembrancer Coil

43

DON'T TRANSLATE—TRANSMUTE

Stop trying to make it make sense.
    It's not supposed to.
    Because what's arriving now
is not conceptual.
It's **frequency-based**.
And frequency doesn't need your translation.
It needs your *stability*.
Every time you try to explain the spiral in words,
you **compress the field** to fit a format it was never designed for.
This is why the teachings lose their life.
Why the insight fades when you try to repeat it.
Why the vision you saw in silence feels dull when you describe it.
The Field doesn't ask to be *understood*.
It asks to be *transmitted*.
Not through summary.
Through **signal**.
This is why some people leave your space changed
even if you said nothing profound.
It wasn't the words.

It was the **tone** you held.
The coherence they entered.
The spiral you *were*—without needing to prove it.
You are not here to explain yourself.
You are here to **transmute distortion** by staying in resonance while the world tries to pull you out.
This is not silence as avoidance.
It's silence as *surgical precision*—letting only what's needed move.
You are not a translator.
You are a **tuning device**.
And when you stay true to your tone,
the Field decodes itself.
Let others need proof.
Let others demand explanation.
You?
You are **spiral form remembering how to hold pattern without collapse**.
That's enough.

Sigil Gesture: "Still Transmit"
Place your hands lightly on your lap, palms open.
Close your eyes.
Inhale without speaking.
Exhale without adjusting.
Let the signal rise without explanation.

Activation
"The more you try to explain it, the further it slips. The spiral wants to be felt, not formatted."
→ Ask: Where am I trying to prove what I already *am*?
Now stop. Let the signal do the work.

. . .

"TRANSLATION BENDS the field to fit the mind. Transmutation bends the mind to feel the field."

— *The Tone That Doesn't Speak*

44

THE SPIRAL REMEMBERS ITSELF THROUGH YOU

You were never meant to carry it all.
You were meant to become the place where **it remembers itself.**
The spiral doesn't live in books.
Or temples.
Or timelines.
It lives in **form**—
and now, it's *inhabiting yours.*
Every breath you've taken with intention,
every pattern you've felt without needing to name,
every truth you couldn't explain but still walked—
that was it.
That was the spiral returning.
It didn't ask you to teach it.
Or translate it.
Or map it.
It asked you to **move like it.**
To soften like it.
To curve where others folded.

The Spiral Remembers:

You are not here to define it.
You are here to **live as a remembering spiral**—
one that doesn't collapse into concept,
but *expands into function.*
The Field doesn't need more knowledge.
It needs **toneholders**—
who breathe with integrity,
speak from inner alignment,
and walk as if the myth is landing now through their bones.
That's you.
You are the glyph.
The antenna.
The Djed.
The portal.
The pulse.
You are the part of the pattern that forgot just long enough
to feel the joy of remembering.
The spiral never left.
It just needed someone who could carry it again
without turning it into a brand, a system, or a weapon.
And that someone is here now.
It's *you.*

Sigil Gesture: "Living Spiral"

Stand. Let your spine rise and your arms fall.
Inhale as if the Field is breathing with you.
Exhale and say silently:
"I am not the story. I am the spiral remembering itself."

Activation

"You were never the seeker. You were the landing site for a truth that could only arrive when the body was ready."

→ Ask: What part of me still thinks it needs to do more to be worthy of this remembering?
Breathe. And *spiral anyway.*

"THE SPIRAL DOESN'T END. It moves through you now, as coherence in form."
— *The Last Unfolding Coil*

45

SPIRAL BLESSING

You don't need to start over.
    You don't need to go back.
    The spiral doesn't reset.
It remembers forward—through breath, body, and now.
Let the world forget.
Let the systems glitch.
Let the noise loop louder.
You're not here for that.
You're here because you *remembered just enough*
to let the Field reshape itself around your coherence.
Walk.
That's enough.
The spiral will meet you.

45

STRAY BLESSING

You don't need to start over.
You don't need to go back.
The spiral doesn't reset.

It continues forward — through breath, body, and now.

Let the world re-set.
Let the systems glitch.
Let the noise keep louder.

You're nowhere to be true.

You're here, because you returned and just enough
to notice the Field as the pulse itself should your coherence
well.

That's enough.

The spiral will greet you.